Castle

HOW IT WORKS

Imprints of Macmillan
175 Fifth Avenue
New York, New York 10010
mackids.com

Printed in China by South China Printing Co. Ltd.,
Dongguan City, Guangdong Province

Square Fish and the Square Fish logo are trademarks
of Macmillan and are used by Roaring Brook Press
under license from Macmillan.

Square Fish logo designed by Filomena Tuosto

Macmillan books may be purchased for business or
promotional use. For information on bulk purchases,
please contact the Macmillan Corporate and Premium
Sales Department at (800) 221-7945 x5442
or by e-mail at specialmarkets@macmillan.com.

Library of Congress Control Number: 2011962160

First Edition: 2013
Second Edition: 2015

ISBN 978-1-62672-208-8 (hardcover)
10 9 8 7 6 5 4 3 2 1

ISBN 978-1-62672-209-5 (paperback)
10 9 8 7 6 5 4 3 2 1

AR: 3.1 / LEXILE: 500L

DAVID MACAULAY

Castle

HOW IT WORKS

with

SHEILA KEENAN

David Macaulay Studio

Roaring Brook Press

New York

The castle stands high
on a rocky hill.
It has tall towers,
thick stone walls,
doors of wood and iron,
and a wide moat.

There is *NO* welcome mat!

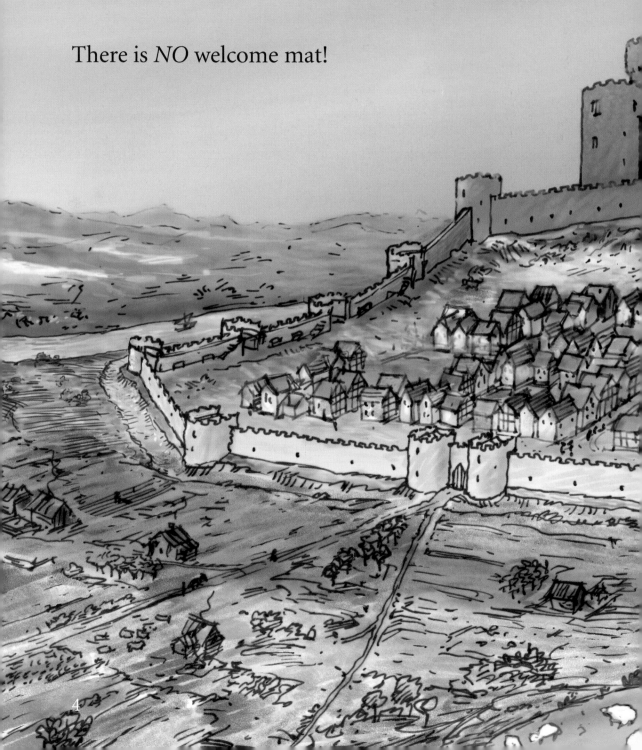

People cannot just walk into a castle.
The castle was built
to keep the people inside safe.
It keeps other people safely outside!

Are you *friend* or *foe*?

If you are a friend
you must first climb a steep ramp.
It ends at a wooden drawbridge.
The drawbridge crosses the moat.
You are now facing the outer wall.
It's called the outer curtain.

You walk toward the first gatehouse.
A tower stands on each side.
Guards decide who can come in.
They watch everyone *very* closely!
Welcome friend!

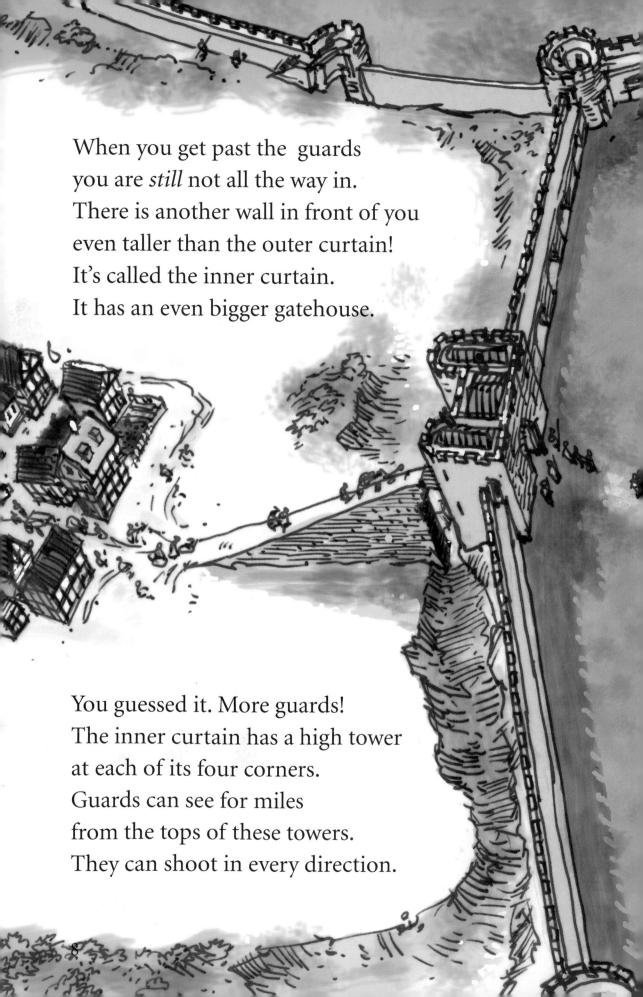

When you get past the guards
you are *still* not all the way in.
There is another wall in front of you
even taller than the outer curtain!
It's called the inner curtain.
It has an even bigger gatehouse.

You guessed it. More guards!
The inner curtain has a high tower
at each of its four corners.
Guards can see for miles
from the tops of these towers.
They can shoot in every direction.

At last! You are deep within the castle.
Welcome to the inner ward.
This courtyard is a lively place!
Horses are fed in the stable
below the barracks.
Soldiers are playing a game.
The blacksmith makes a new horseshoe.

The blacksmith's children are chasing chickens.
The cook builds a big fire in the kitchen.
The cook's helper draws water from the well.
He must water the garden.
The dog gets a drink, too.

The lord and lady live in one of the high towers.
The walls of these rooms are painted.
Fresh herbs are tossed on the floors.
This makes the rooms smell good.

A spiral staircase goes all the way to the roof.
Guards keep watch from the walls
and towers day and night.

The ground floor is filled with dried food
and barrels of wine and cider.
Beneath the ground floor is
the dark, damp dungeon.

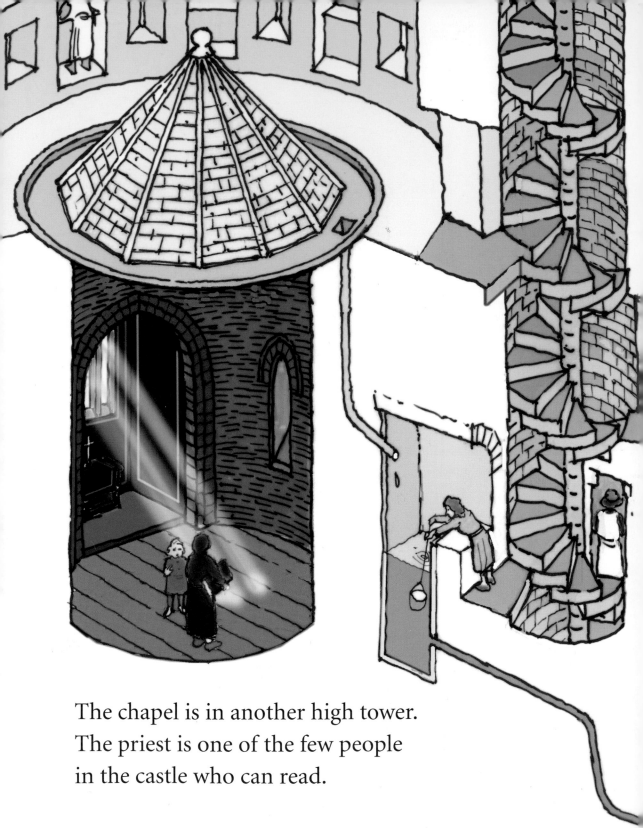

The chapel is in another high tower.
The priest is one of the few people
in the castle who can read.

The roof above the chapel collects rainwater.
It flows through a pipe into a tank
and then all the way down to the kitchen sink.

14

A guard has stopped to use the toilet.
Listen! Can you hear his teeth chattering?
He sits over a hole
cut into a cold stone slab.
Below the hole is a shaft
that goes down to a pit.
The knight uses hay for toilet paper.

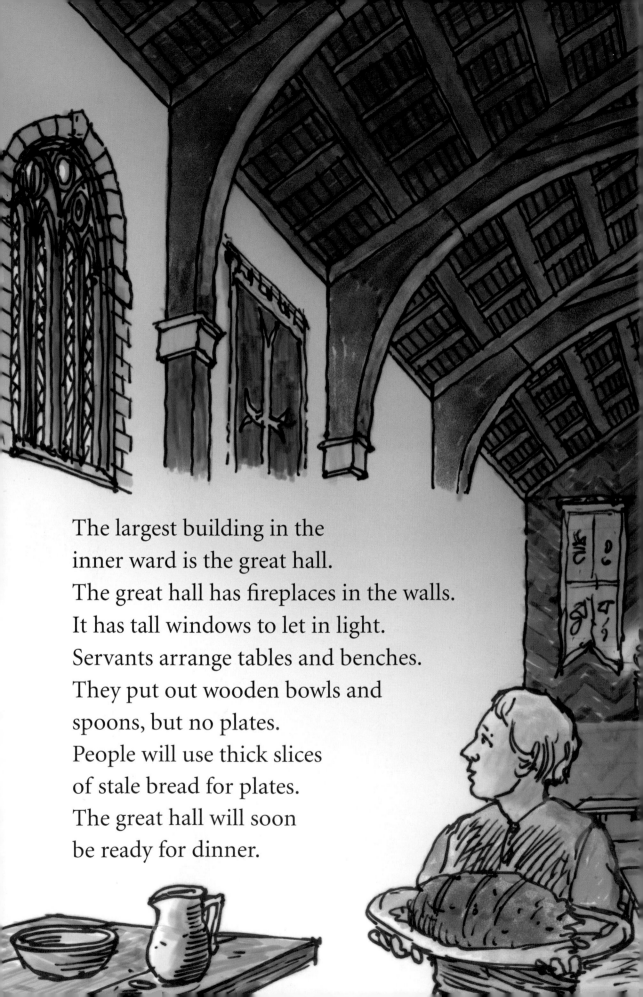

The largest building in the
inner ward is the great hall.
The great hall has fireplaces in the walls.
It has tall windows to let in light.
Servants arrange tables and benches.
They put out wooden bowls and
spoons, but no plates.
People will use thick slices
of stale bread for plates.
The great hall will soon
be ready for dinner.

If you are a foe, or an enemy,
you won't be let in.
To capture the castle
you will have to surround it and wait.
This is called a siege.
A siege stops supplies
from getting into the castle.

But you'd better be patient. Remember
all the dried food
in the towers?
And don't forget the water in the well.
Your army may surround the castle,
but the people inside can last
a long time.

Are you in a hurry?
You'll have to get past
the town wall first.
Bring on the battering ram!

The battering ram hangs by chains
inside a wooden shed.
You swing it back and forth.

It hits the wall hard!

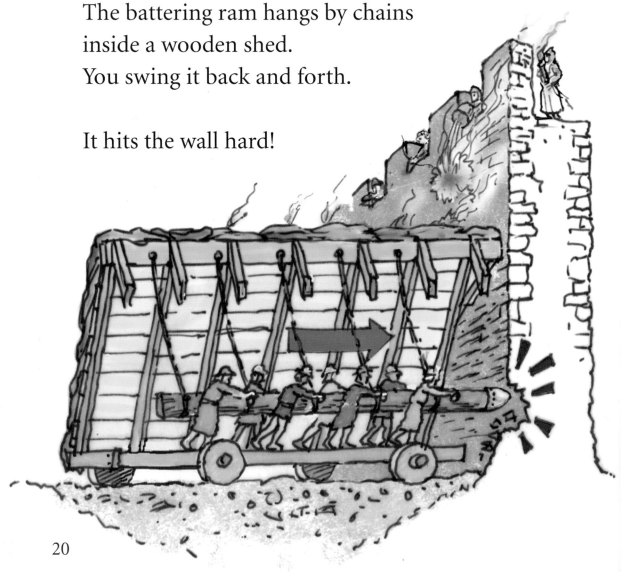

If you make a big enough hole,
you can crawl through it.
Now you can open the gatehouse doors
and let your soldiers in.

But the soldiers inside
can see you coming.
Guards remove the supports
under the drawbridge.
One end flips up,
the other end drops down.
No more bridge!

You could wheel in a catapult.
It looks like a giant wooden spoon.
You can fire big heavy rocks.
You can also fire smelly,
germy dead animals.
Fire! *Whoosh!* Pigs away!

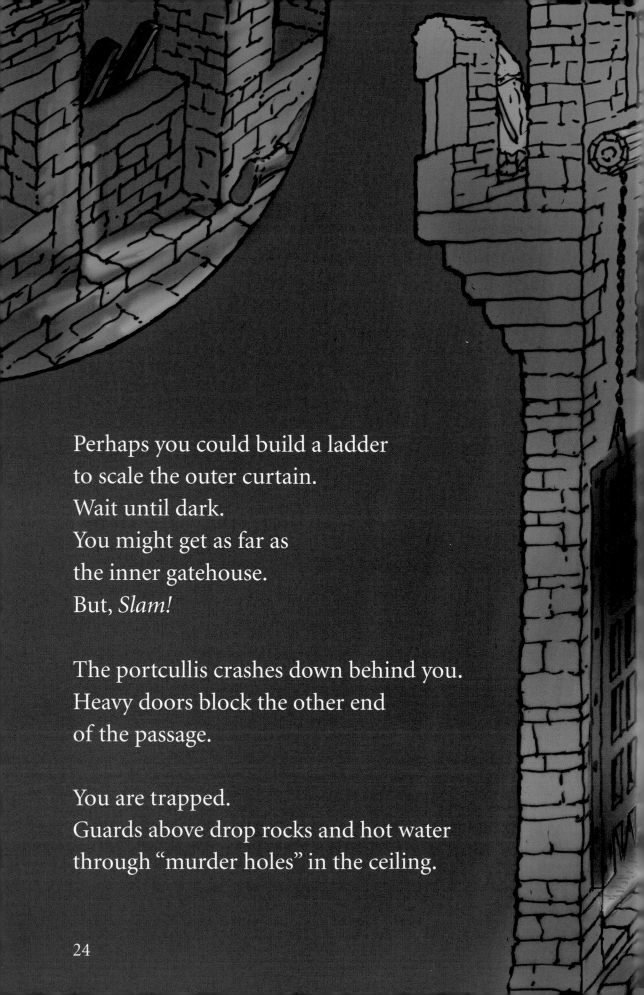

Perhaps you could build a ladder
to scale the outer curtain.
Wait until dark.
You might get as far as
the inner gatehouse.
But, *Slam!*

The portcullis crashes down behind you.
Heavy doors block the other end
of the passage.

You are trapped.
Guards above drop rocks and hot water
through "murder holes" in the ceiling.

If you do get through this gatehouse,
there are many more soldiers waiting.
They patrol the battlements along the tops
of all the walls and towers.
Archers will greet you with flaming arrows.

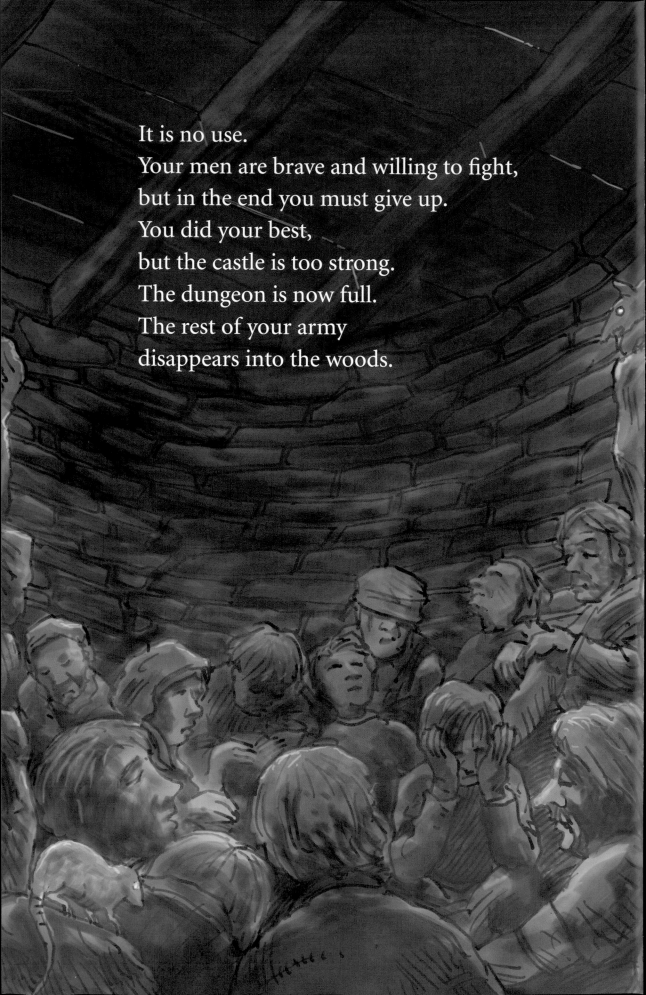

It is no use.
Your men are brave and willing to fight,
but in the end you must give up.
You did your best,
but the castle is too strong.
The dungeon is now full.
The rest of your army
disappears into the woods.

Slowly, the inner ward comes back to life.
The mess will be cleaned up tomorrow.
Tonight there will be a celebration.
The cook has put away his bow and arrows
and grabbed a spoon.
Bring on the meat, beans, onions, and puddings.
And please don't forget the eel pie!

Words To Know

archer someone who shoots with a bow and arrow or crossbow

barracks a building where soldiers live

battering ram a heavy wooden beam or log that is rammed against enemy walls

battlement the top of a castle wall

blacksmith someone who makes and fits horseshoes and mends things made of iron

catapult a weapon used for firing things over castle walls

drawbridge a bridge than can be raised and lowered

dungeon an underground prison

foe an enemy

gatehouse a fortified entryway often protected by a portcullis

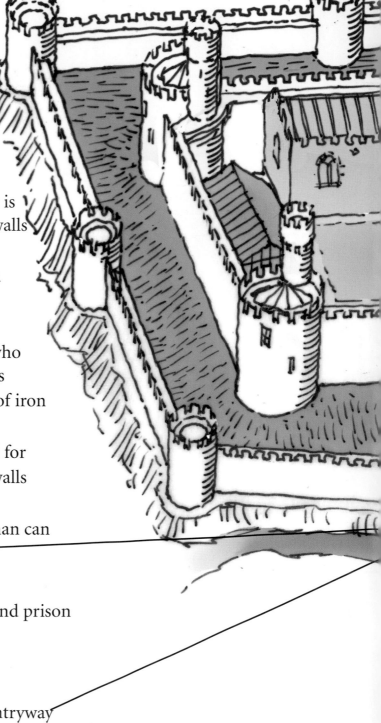

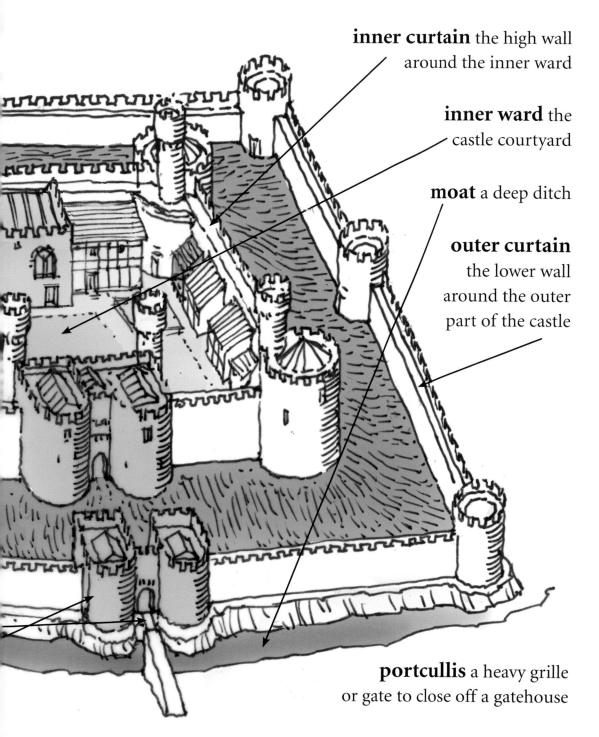

inner curtain the high wall around the inner ward

inner ward the castle courtyard

moat a deep ditch

outer curtain the lower wall around the outer part of the castle

portcullis a heavy grille or gate to close off a gatehouse

siege surrounding a castle to make those inside surrender

spiral a pattern that winds around in circles

To Learn More

Built To Last by David Macaulay. Houghton Mifflin Harcourt, 2010.
Castles by Stephanie Turnbull, illustrated by Colin King. Usborne, 2007.

Castle (DVD), hosted by David Macaulay, PBS Home Video, 2006.

www.castles.org
This site shows castles from all over the world.
There is a link to children's pages. There is also a list of castles for sale!

http://www.neuschwanstein.de
Click the second flag from the left for English.
The Sleeping Beauty castle in Disneyland was inspired by this real castle in Germany!
The site also has a children's page with games.

Index